W9-CPW-731

This book
belongs to

....

ZIGZAG FACTFINDERS

MONSTER ANIMALS

Written by
Gerald Legg

Edited by
Nicola Wright

zigzag

Gerald Legg PhD FRES FZS is Keeper of Biology at the Booth Museum of Natural History, Brighton, England, where he regularly talks to children about all types of animals.

ZIGZAG PUBLISHING

Published by Zigzag Publishing,
a division of Quadrillion Publishing Ltd.,
Godalming Business Centre, Woolsack Way,
Godalming, Surrey GU7 1XW, England.

Series concept: Tony Potter
Design Manager: Kate Buxton
Designed by: Chris Leishman
Illustrated by: Peter Bull, Steven Young, Clive Pritchard, Treve Tamblin and John Yates
Cover illustration: Tony Karpinski

Color separations: Scan Trans, Singapore
Printed in Singapore

Distributed in the U.S. by SMITHMARK PUBLISHERS
a division of U.S. Media Holdings, Inc.,
16 East 32nd Street, New York, NY 10016

Copyright © 1997 Zigzag Publishing. First published 1994.

All rights reserved. No part of this publication may be reproduced, stored in a retrieval system or transmitted by any means, electronic, mechanical, photocopying or otherwise, without the prior permission of the publisher.

ISBN 0-7651-9317-5
8043

Contents

About this book

This book introduces you to the fiercest, scariest, weirdest and deadliest monsters of the animal kingdom. Find out which are the biggest monsters on land, in the air and under the sea. You can also see the fattest, hairiest and most disgusting monsters around!

Many of these animals only look monstrous in order to protect themselves from attack by other animals. Most animals like to be left alone and will only act fiercely in self-defence.

There are plenty of fearsome imaginary monsters - some of which may even exist! Discover too, some of the truly monstrous animals that used to roam the Earth, but are now extinct.

Pythons swallow their prey whole.

Happily there are few really monstrous large animals. Smaller monsters are much more common.

Giant **pythons** coil their powerful bodies around their helpless prey until they suffocate it.

Many large animals might look frightening, but usually they do not attack unless they are threatened.

The **elephant** is the largest land mammal. A full grown male (bull) African elephant can be over 10 ft. tall and weigh 9 tons.

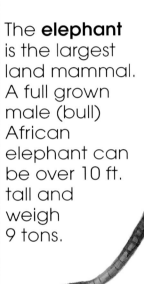

The enormous **Komodo Dragon** prowls through the forest on lonely Indonesian islands.

This fierce lizard, nearly three metres long, will even attack people.

A **tiger** has huge, sharp teeth which grip and kill its prey.

The **giraffe** is the tallest mammal on Earth. However, it is not fierce and eats only leaves.

Grizzly bears tower a frightening 10 ft. when they stand upright on their hind legs. They have big, sharp claws for tearing at food.

Gorillas are the largest primates. When threatened, a male gorilla will beat his chest with his hands, roar and rush toward the enemy.

The **Goliath beetle** is a heavy weight champion of the insect world. It can carry a load 850 times its own weight. That is similar to a human carrying 67 tons.

Some of the strangest monsters can be found swimming and living in the sea.

Large ones like the whales and sharks swim in the open ocean. Others, like giant sponges, hide deep down on the seabed.

Lurking at the bottom of the sea near Japan are **giant spider crabs**. With their claws outstretched they can measure nearly ten feet.

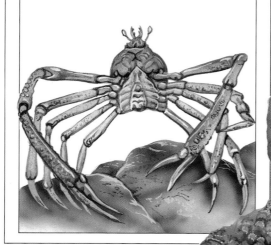

The suckers on a 50 foot **giant squid** measure 4 in. across. But sucker scars on whales have been seen as long as 18 in.!

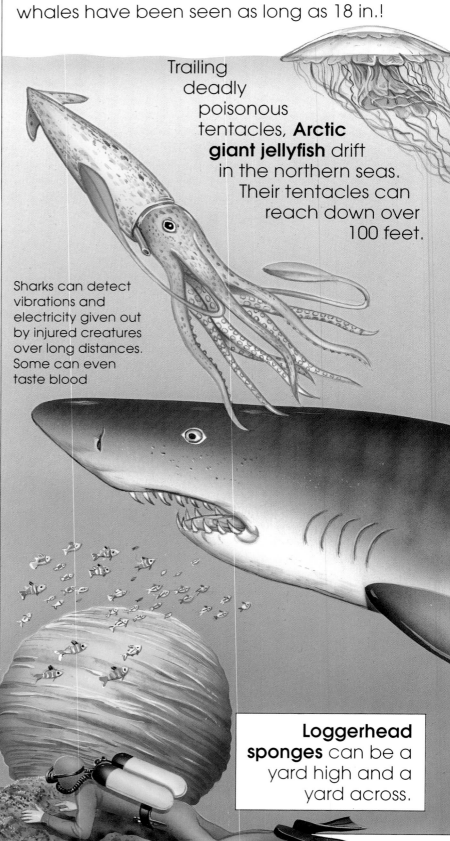

Trailing deadly poisonous tentacles, **Arctic giant jellyfish** drift in the northern seas. Their tentacles can reach down over 100 feet.

Sharks can detect vibrations and electricity given out by injured creatures over long distances. Some can even taste blood

Loggerhead sponges can be a yard high and a yard across.

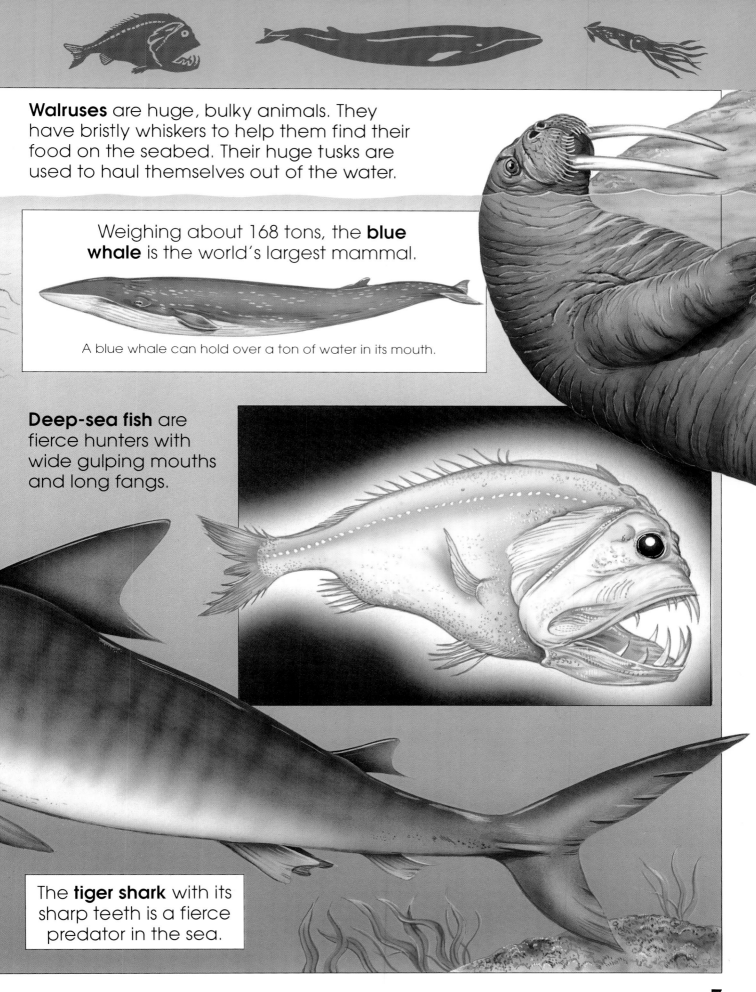

Walruses are huge, bulky animals. They have bristly whiskers to help them find their food on the seabed. Their huge tusks are used to haul themselves out of the water.

Weighing about 168 tons, the **blue whale** is the world's largest mammal.

A blue whale can hold over a ton of water in its mouth.

Deep-sea fish are fierce hunters with wide gulping mouths and long fangs.

The **tiger shark** with its sharp teeth is a fierce predator in the sea.

Monsters in the air

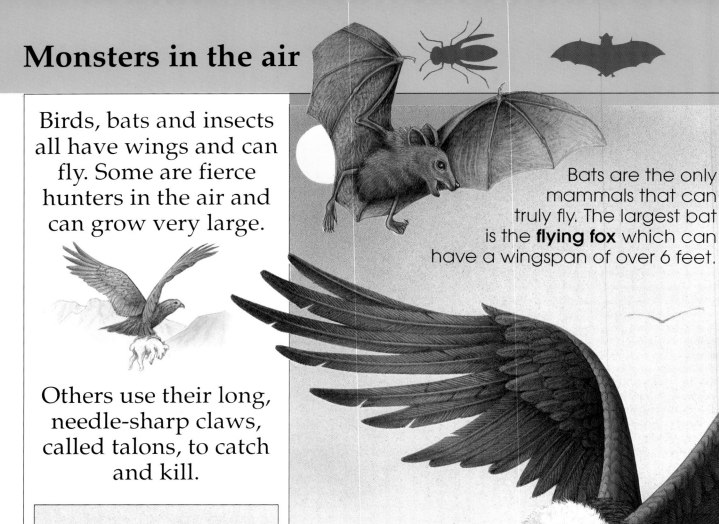

Birds, bats and insects all have wings and can fly. Some are fierce hunters in the air and can grow very large.

Others use their long, needle-sharp claws, called talons, to catch and kill.

Monstrous **robber flies** hunt other insects in the air, piercing them with sharp mouthpieces, and sucking out the contents of their bodies.

Bats are the only mammals that can truly fly. The largest bat is the **flying fox** which can have a wingspan of over 6 feet.

The **Andean condor** is the world's largest bird of prey and can weigh over 25 lbs.

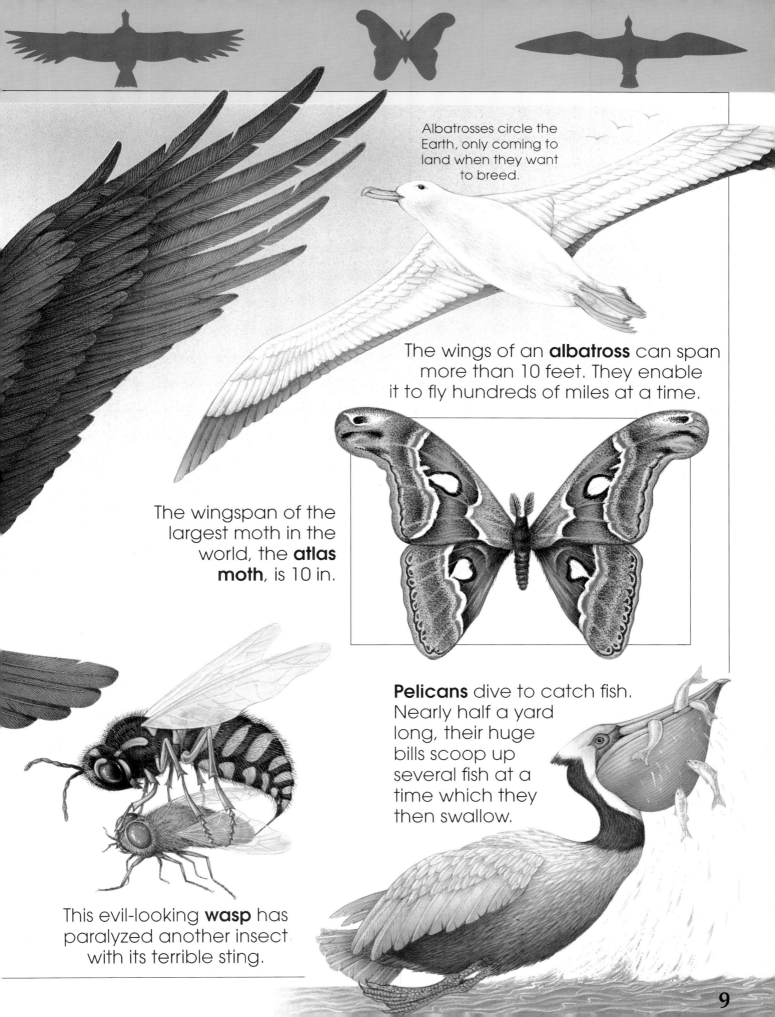

Albatrosses circle the Earth, only coming to land when they want to breed.

The wings of an **albatross** can span more than 10 feet. They enable it to fly hundreds of miles at a time.

The wingspan of the largest moth in the world, the **atlas moth**, is 10 in.

Pelicans dive to catch fish. Nearly half a yard long, their huge bills scoop up several fish at a time which they then swallow.

This evil-looking **wasp** has paralyzed another insect with its terrible sting.

9

Hairy monsters

Monster animals covered with hair can look very strange. They are hairy for many reasons.

Some live in very cold places and need to keep warm. Others use hair for camouflage.

Poisonous hairs protect against attack. Hairs are even used to help some animals breathe underwater.

The hairs on this **Japanese Dictyoploca moth caterpillar** irritate and hurt any predator trying to eat it.

The body of a **porcupine** is covered with special hairs. When frightened the animal rattles these needle-sharp quills.

Some porcupines can even shoot quills out at their enemy.

The "old man of the forest," or **orang-utang**, has very long, golden red hair.

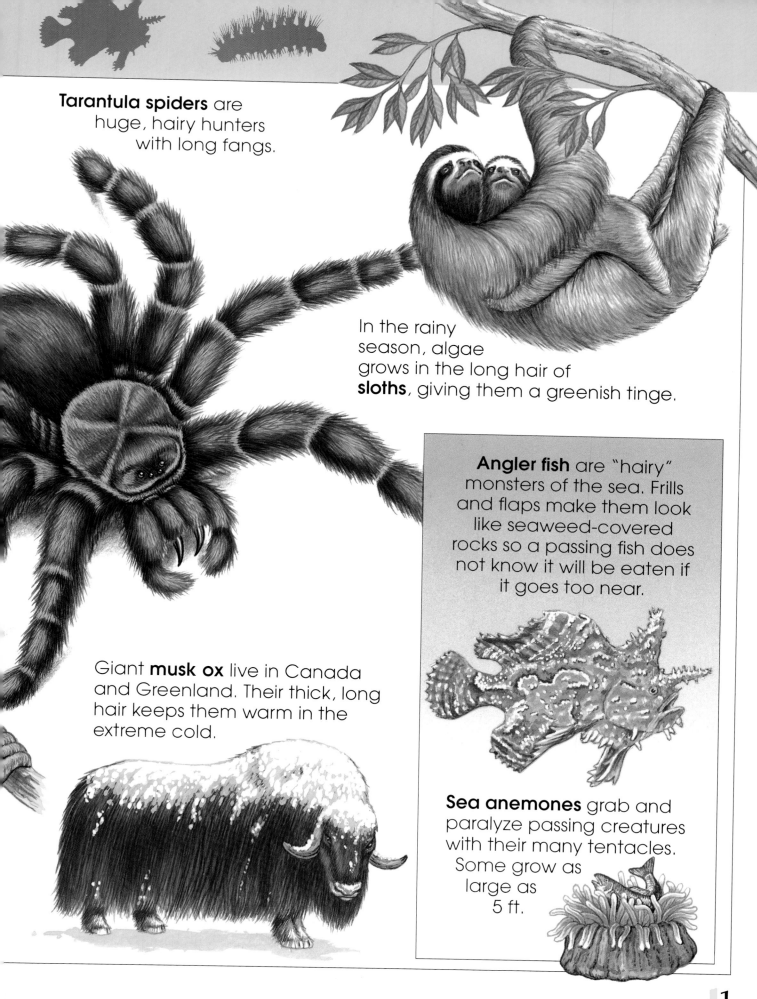

Tarantula spiders are huge, hairy hunters with long fangs.

In the rainy season, algae grows in the long hair of **sloths**, giving them a greenish tinge.

Angler fish are "hairy" monsters of the sea. Frills and flaps make them look like seaweed-covered rocks so a passing fish does not know it will be eaten if it goes too near.

Giant **musk ox** live in Canada and Greenland. Their thick, long hair keeps them warm in the extreme cold.

Sea anemones grab and paralyze passing creatures with their many tentacles. Some grow as large as 5 ft.

To protect themselves from being attacked or eaten, many animals are monstrous looking.

Some look frightening all the time, while others can make themselves scary when they have to.

Roaring and puffing up their bodies are just some of the methods used.

Death's head hawkmoths can enter beehives and steal honey without being stung.

The strange skull-like markings on the **death's head hawkmoth** give it a deathly appearance.

This is not a fierce prehistoric monster, but a **frilled lizard**. This harmless lizard puts on an impressive display when it is frightened.

Male **stag beetles** have huge, fearsome jaws. They cannot bite with them, but instead joust with other males over females.

Stag beetles use their huge jaws to try and flick their opponent over.

14

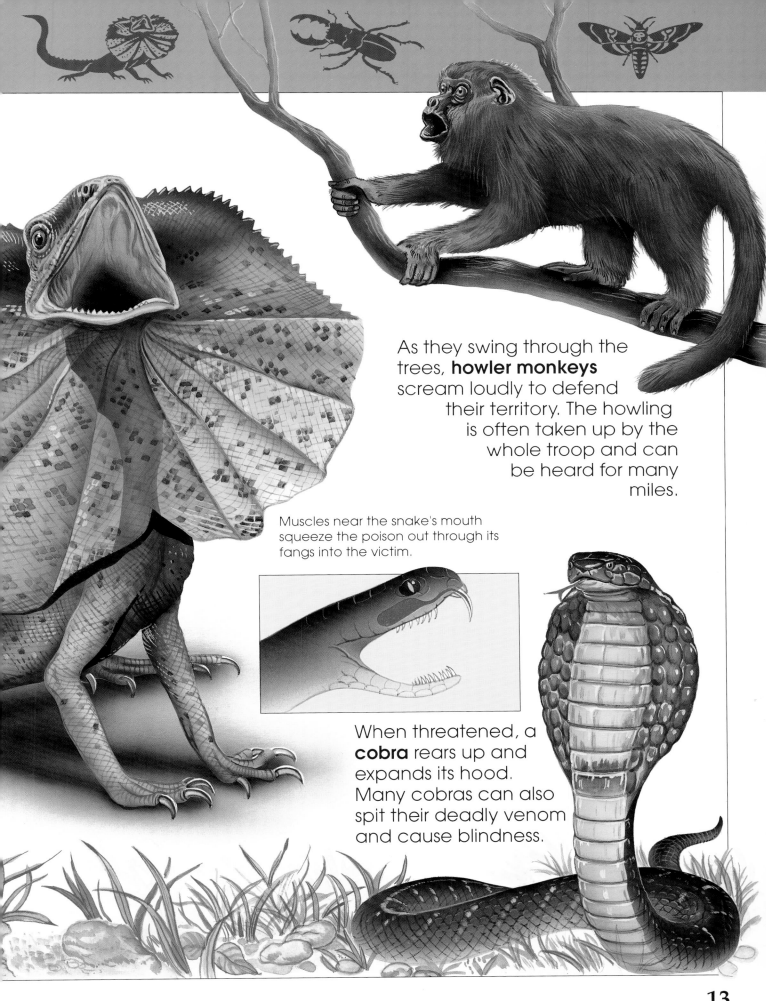

As they swing through the trees, **howler monkeys** scream loudly to defend their territory. The howling is often taken up by the whole troop and can be heard for many miles.

Muscles near the snake's mouth squeeze the poison out through its fangs into the victim.

When threatened, a **cobra** rears up and expands its hood. Many cobras can also spit their deadly venom and cause blindness.

Disgusting monsters

Some monster animals use horrid smells to frighten their predators.

Others live in smelly places or have disgusting habits.

Eating dung and rotting corpses is not particularly nice, but without these animals to clear up, the world would be even smellier!

Big dung beetles carefully roll dung into balls which they hide in tunnels underground for their grubs to eat.

When a **vampire bat** finds a sleeping animal, it bites into the skin with its razor-sharp front teeth and laps up the blood with its tongue.

Vultures have bald heads and necks. This stops them from getting too dirty with blood as they poke their heads inside a corpse to feed.

Lampreys cling to other fish with their strange circular mouths surrounded by hooks. They gnaw the flesh and even wriggle into their host's body.

Leeches attach themselves to animals and suck blood causing their bodies to swell. Some can grow as long as 8 in.

Flies are attracted to dead bodies where they feed and lay their eggs. Once hatched, the maggots help to break down the rotten flesh.

Phew! The pungent odor of a **skunk** is disgusting. Skunks spray their scent to mark their territory and put off attackers.

Fierce Monsters

Many animals are hunters, preying on other creatures. To catch and kill they have to be cunning, powerful and quick. Most have special teeth, jaws and stings to help catch, hold, kill and devour their victims.

Some of these fierce monsters are quite small. Others grow enormous and will even attack and eat people.

Giant **Colombian horned toads** are aggressive and will attack animals much bigger than themselves - they even bite horses!

Over a thousand people a year are killed by the world's largest and fiercest crocodile, the **Indo-Pacific crocodile**.

A **scorpion** grabs its prey with sharp claws and then bends its tail with its deadly sting over its head and into the victim, killing it with the poison.

Using their razor-sharp pointed teeth, **killer whales** can snatch a seal from a beach by rushing on to the shore on a wave. People stranded on ice floes have also been tipped off and eaten.

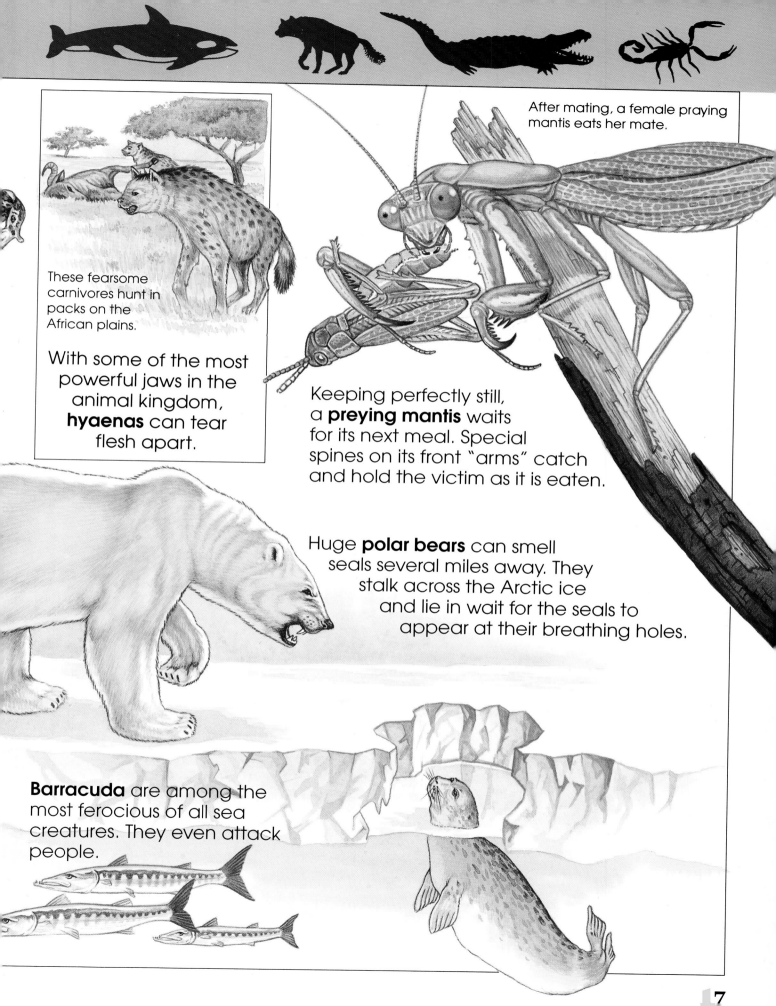

After mating, a female praying mantis eats her mate.

These fearsome carnivores hunt in packs on the African plains.

With some of the most powerful jaws in the animal kingdom, **hyaenas** can tear flesh apart.

Keeping perfectly still, a **preying mantis** waits for its next meal. Special spines on its front "arms" catch and hold the victim as it is eaten.

Huge **polar bears** can smell seals several miles away. They stalk across the Arctic ice and lie in wait for the seals to appear at their breathing holes.

Barracuda are among the most ferocious of all sea creatures. They even attack people.

Fat monsters

Some animals are monstrously fat. Many of them spend most of their time in the water where the weight of their bodies is supported.

Fat bodies can hold a lot of food for times when there is little food around. They can also be used to scare off attackers.

The fat **Vietnamese pot-bellied pig** is kept as a pet in some parts of the world.

Herds of **elephant seals** wallow on the beach. An adult male can weigh almost four tons. When males fight each other they often crush the babies on the beach.

Hippopotamus means "river horse." Although they look fat and clumsy on land, when they are in water they can swim fast.

Hippos use their large teeth for digging up water plants and fighting.

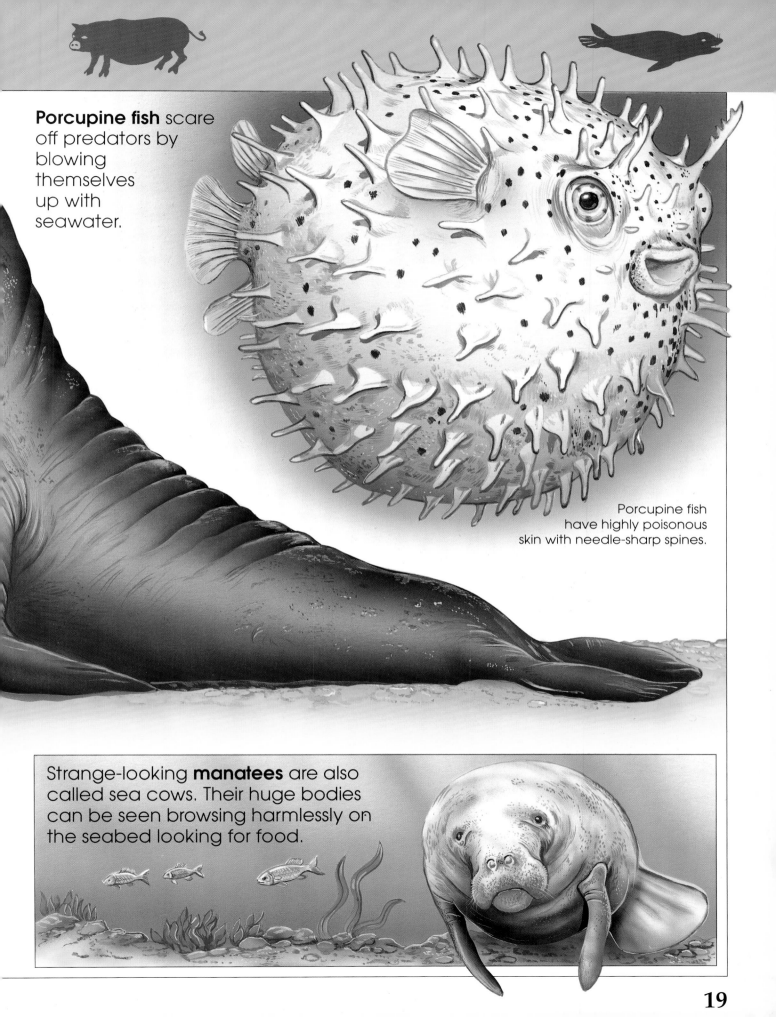

Porcupine fish scare off predators by blowing themselves up with seawater.

Porcupine fish have highly poisonous skin with needle-sharp spines.

Strange-looking **manatees** are also called sea cows. Their huge bodies can be seen browsing harmlessly on the seabed looking for food.

Weird monsters

Some animals are very strange-looking to us. But these monsters are usually the shape they are for a reason.

Everything is made so that it is suited to where it lives so it can survive.

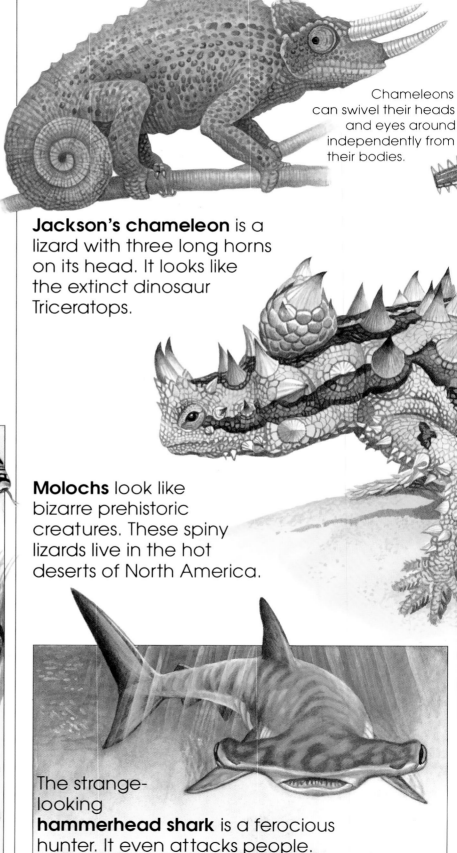

Chameleons can swivel their heads and eyes around independently from their bodies.

Jackson's chameleon is a lizard with three long horns on its head. It looks like the extinct dinosaur Triceratops.

Molochs look like bizarre prehistoric creatures. These spiny lizards live in the hot deserts of North America.

Animals do not usually have two heads, but sometimes they are born. This freak two-headed **kingsnake** was found in California.

The strange-looking **hammerhead shark** is a ferocious hunter. It even attacks people.

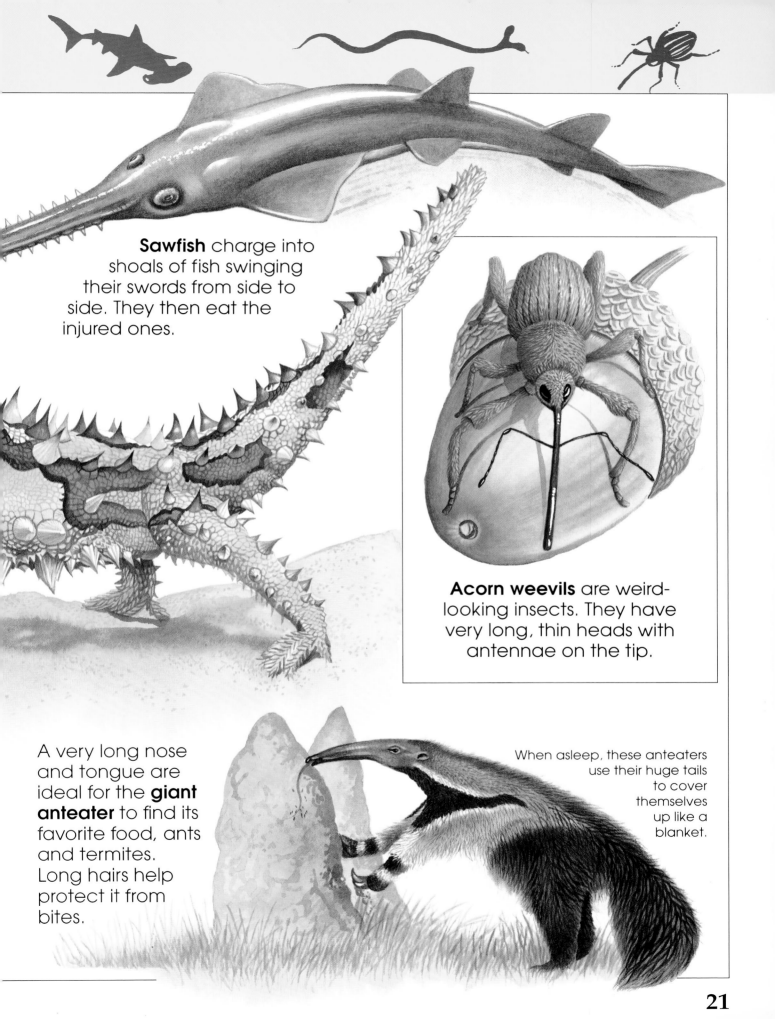

Sawfish charge into shoals of fish swinging their swords from side to side. They then eat the injured ones.

Acorn weevils are weird-looking insects. They have very long, thin heads with antennae on the tip.

A very long nose and tongue are ideal for the **giant anteater** to find its favorite food, ants and termites. Long hairs help protect it from bites.

When asleep, these anteaters use their huge tails to cover themselves up like a blanket.

Deadly monsters

Many animals protect themselves from attack by stinging or biting.

Some animals use poison to stun or kill their prey. Many of these deadly animals have ways of warning others to keep away!

A **black widow spider** traps its prey in a web and then sucks out its insides.

Long, brightly colored spines cover the body of the beautiful but deadly **lion fish**. The sharp spines are coated with toxic mucus and cause terrible pain if touched.

The long trailing tentacles of the **Portuguese Man O'War jellyfish** are highly poisonous. Stinging cells shoot tiny barbed harpoons into anything that touches them.

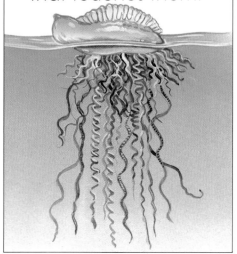

The bright colors of **poison dart frogs** warn predators to leave them alone.

People living in the rainforests of South America smear their blow-pipe darts with the frog's mucus (slime) to poison their prey.

Many **sea urchins** are covered in sharp, poisonous spines for protection. If stepped on the spines can stab and break off in your foot.

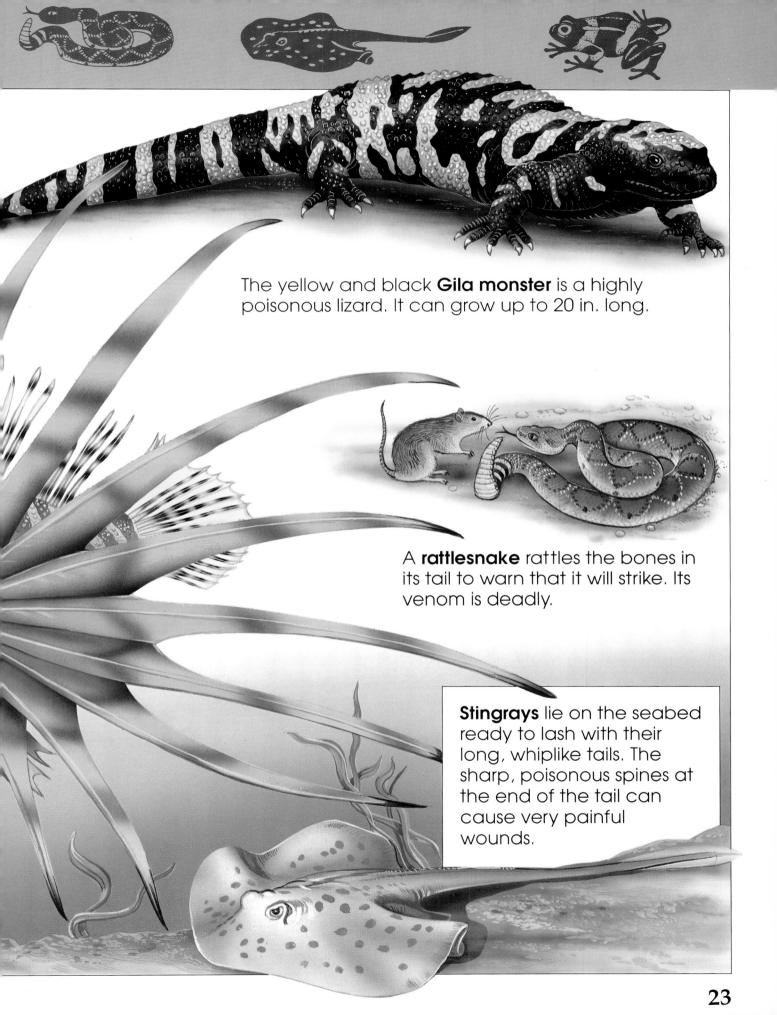

The yellow and black **Gila monster** is a highly poisonous lizard. It can grow up to 20 in. long.

A **rattlesnake** rattles the bones in its tail to warn that it will strike. Its venom is deadly.

Stingrays lie on the seabed ready to lash with their long, whiplike tails. The sharp, poisonous spines at the end of the tail can cause very painful wounds.

23

Some animals are only frightening and dangerous in large numbers.

Some, like bees, live together in groups to help each other. Others, like wolves, hunt in packs.

Some animals only group together in masses at certain times.

In some parts of the world, plagues of flying **locusts** can darken the sky, eating every green plant they land on.

Hornets live as a colony, nesting inside hollow trees. They use their huge jaws and deadly sting to hunt.

A colony of **army ants** marching through the forest will eat everything in its way - even small animals.

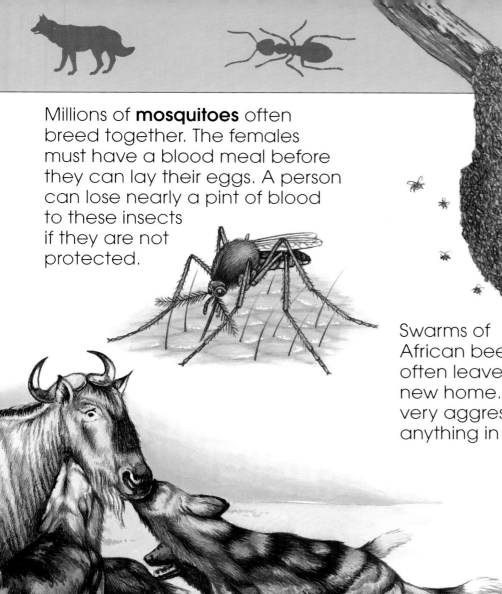

Millions of **mosquitoes** often breed together. The females must have a blood meal before they can lay their eggs. A person can lose nearly a pint of blood to these insects if they are not protected.

Swarms of African bees often leave their hive to find a new home. These **"killer bees"** are very aggressive and will attack anything in their way.

African wild dogs live in packs of up to 60. By circling their prey and dashing in and biting it, the victim is soon weakened and killed.

Hunting together in packs, **wolves** can catch and kill large animals. They usually attack the weak and sick, but rarely people.

Rare monsters

Many animals are becoming rare. Some have already become extinct and will never be seen again outside a museum.

People kill animals for their skin, fur, feathers and horns. We also destroy the places where they live.

The largest **false scorpion** in Europe lives under the bark of dead trees. It is now extremely rare and only found in ancient forests.

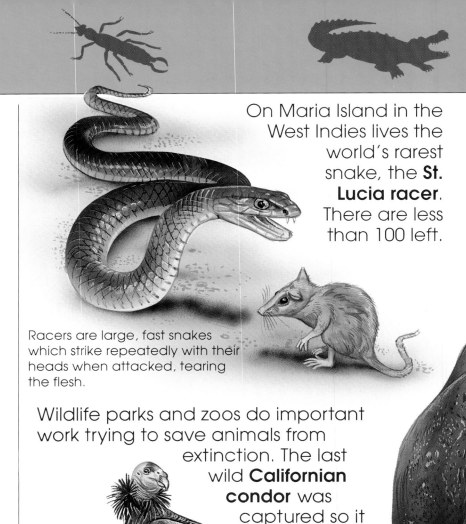

Racers are large, fast snakes which strike repeatedly with their heads when attacked, tearing the flesh.

On Maria Island in the West Indies lives the world's rarest snake, the **St. Lucia racer**. There are less than 100 left.

Wildlife parks and zoos do important work trying to save animals from extinction. The last wild **Californian condor** was captured so it could breed under protection.

Trap door spiders in Southeast Asia are the rarest spiders. They use their jaws to dig holes, leaving a hinged lid at the entrance. When a victim comes near, the spider opens the lid, grabs its prey, and pulls it underground.

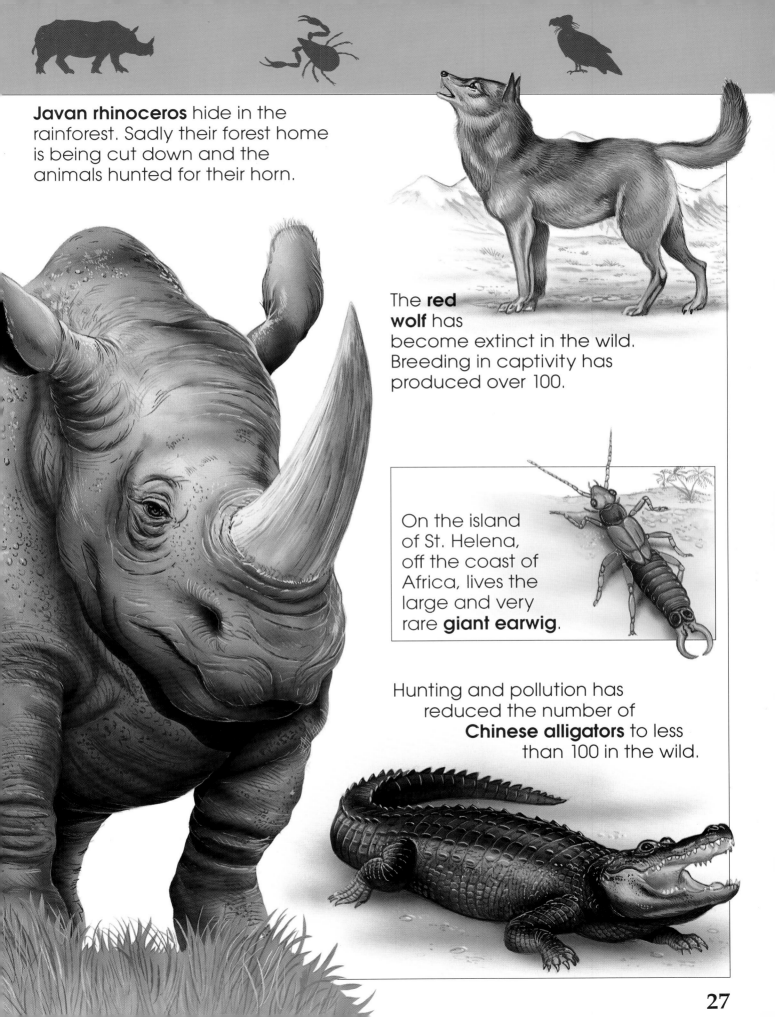

Javan rhinoceros hide in the rainforest. Sadly their forest home is being cut down and the animals hunted for their horn.

The **red wolf** has become extinct in the wild. Breeding in captivity has produced over 100.

On the island of St. Helena, off the coast of Africa, lives the large and very rare **giant earwig**.

Hunting and pollution has reduced the number of **Chinese alligators** to less than 100 in the wild.

Imaginary monsters

Superstition and fear have made people dream up all kinds of strange and imaginary monsters.

Some of these unnatural creatures were invented from stories of unusual animals brought back by travelers.

Other mythical monsters are based on actual living, and extinct, animals.

Some imaginary monsters might be real, we just do not know for sure.

Every year, thousands of people watch the water on Loch Ness in Scotland, hoping to see the **Loch Ness Monster**. Some believe that the monster could be a surviving plesiosaur, a prehistoric sea creature.

The **hydra** is a nine-headed beast of Greek mythology. It was very difficult to kill as each time a head was cut off it grew two new ones.

Sailors' sightings of mermaids may have been **dugongs**. At a distance, female dugongs with their young look like women holding their babies in their arms.

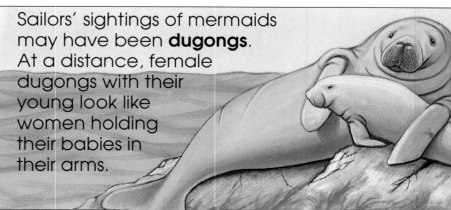

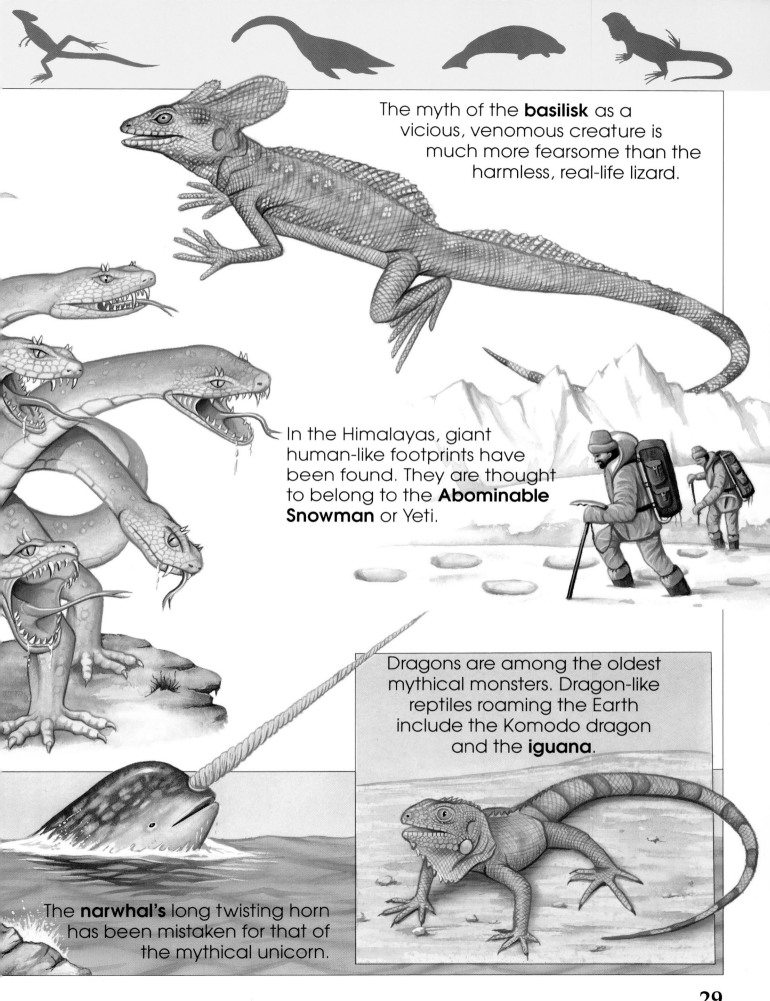

The myth of the **basilisk** as a vicious, venomous creature is much more fearsome than the harmless, real-life lizard.

In the Himalayas, giant human-like footprints have been found. They are thought to belong to the **Abominable Snowman** or Yeti.

Dragons are among the oldest mythical monsters. Dragon-like reptiles roaming the Earth include the Komodo dragon and the **iguana**.

The **narwhal's** long twisting horn has been mistaken for that of the mythical unicorn.

Millions of years ago, all kinds of strange monstrous animals roamed the Earth.

There were no people around when the dinosaurs ruled the world.

When people appeared they cut down forests and hunted animals. Some of the larger species were driven into extinction. Today, people still kill and threaten many animals.

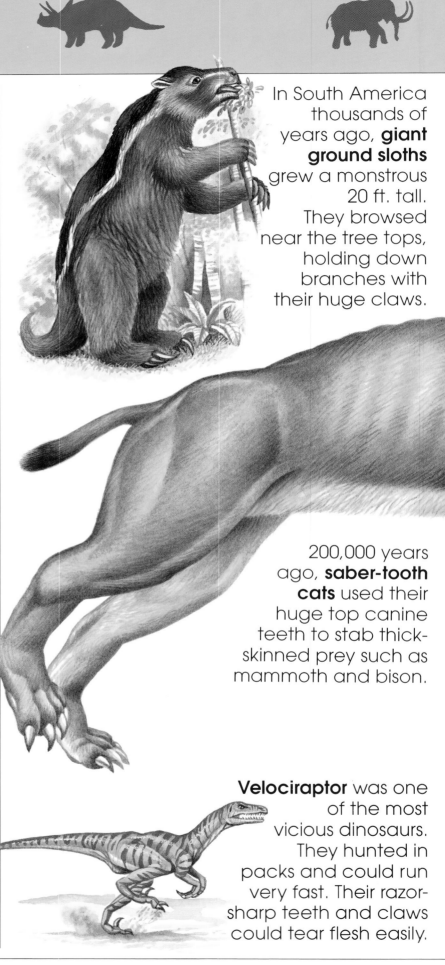

In South America thousands of years ago, **giant ground sloths** grew a monstrous 20 ft. tall. They browsed near the tree tops, holding down branches with their huge claws.

200,000 years ago, **saber-tooth cats** used their huge top canine teeth to stab thick-skinned prey such as mammoth and bison.

Velociraptor was one of the most vicious dinosaurs. They hunted in packs and could run very fast. Their razor-sharp teeth and claws could tear flesh easily.

Quetzalcoatlus' wings were made of skin like those of bats today.

97 million years ago, **quetzalcoatlus** soared through the air on wings spanning 40 feet.

Giant Irish deer grew antlers nearly 13 feet across. They died out 2,500 years ago.

Mammoths are one of the largest land mammals to have lived. They grew over 13 ft. tall and had woolly coats and huge tusks.

The giant **moa** of New Zealand was the tallest bird that ever existed. It stood over 10 feet tall.

Hyaenodon must have been a fearsome hunter and scavenger. Its skull was 26 in. long and full of needle-sharp teeth.

People destroyed the moa's habitat and hunted it, so that by 1800 it was extinct.

31

 # Index